A Peak In My

Window

FRANCES WILSON

EXPRESSO
331 Newman Springs Road,
Red Bank, New Jersey, 07701
1-888-251-6088 ext 101
info@expressopublishing.com

In loving, and cherished memory of my mother, Izzie, Cinderella Wilson, who opened and helped me manage my first window on the world.

Also, in grateful memory of school teachers, Sunday school teachers, and Youth leaders who helped to show me the way, especially through what they said.

With Special thanks to family who encouraged me by listening. Your frowns, scowls, puzzled looks, and outright laughs, ascertained correctness in the situations I recalled. Also, to friends who encouraged me to chase my dream, many times when it seemed to evade me.

"People who need people, are the luckiest people of all"[1], one singer opines. She's correct, we need each other. We're all sojourners, and despite our varied differences, we share a common path – something we cannot avoid.

We're all givers and takers. Everyone of us has something to offer, and we all need something from each other. We do not all need the same things, nor do we need them to the same extent, yet we all need help, and can offer help.

Some may debate the fact, that often we help much through our words. Reality supports it. Many people live in poverty, so cannot offer material things. Others are not in need of material things.

We can all, however, help in some way. We can for instance, boost morale, challenge, or stimulate even one person to probably change a mindset: get back on the right track – through our words. That can have a ripple effect. It worked in the past. It can still work.

We, therefore, need sensitivity and wisdom. Like it is with other situations, it may not happen with naturalness nor ease. It can, in fact, be a task, but it is a possibility.

A king offers advice: "To make an apt answer is a joy to a man, and a word spoken in season, how good it is."[2] "A word fitly spoken is like apples of gold in a setting of silver."[3]

Almost everyone has at least one, these days. They're so much a part of our lives; we can't imagine having none. Some people have more than others, and the types that boast qualities, are out of reach for some who would like to own them. The number, and the type, however, do not matter.

What matters is ownership and use. Another importance is knowing how to use, manage, and adjust them. Opening them creates a force we may, or may not be able to control. On the other hand, not opening them, creates another kind of force. Experience proves that opening them can bring and increase satisfaction. We just need to open them with caution.

They present the world to us in many ways. Others looking at ours, collect, amass, process and use information. We do the same. Sometimes during sifting, and in many cases during collection, we may misinterpret some of the information. This can breed misunderstanding, which can foster wrong assumptions.

Without correction, wrong assumptions promote conclusions, abort friendships, and perpetuate isolation and alienation. Maintaining them demands much effort, yet it's a must. We cannot do life without them. We must continually clean and adjust them for optimum use, for ourselves and for others.

Chapter 1

A glance at windows

I wonder how you would feel if you had to stay inside for two days, without a chance to go outside.

It depends? On what does it depend?

As long as you can glance outside at least once a day, it would be okay? There's fairness in that.

It is not a problem for you?

Okay. You who say it is not a problem. What if you were in a building without any window?

Abandon that imagination – for the moment. Stop hyperventilating. Breathe – from your diaphragm.

Windows abound, and except for meat smoking shacks, every building has at least one. This was not always the case. History informs us that primitive homes had none. Industry as we know it, was not in existence then. If the assault continues, glance at a window nearby. Without them, life would abound with maladjustment, like the one you just demonstrated. No windows, no life, or life without quality.

The market teems with choices like sizes, and with styles like Fixed, Sliding, Picture, Skylight, Storm, to name just a few. They also vary in cost. Consumers get their money's worth, and this can be harsh reality, for many who cannot afford high quality.

Although we may take them for granted, windows have significance. The term, in fact, has several definitions:

"An opening in a wall, door, roof, or vehicle, that allows the passage or air and light, and if not closed or sealed, air and sound."[4]

"An opening in a wall, or roof, that allows light or air into an enclosure, and often opening or closing."[5]

Windows have advanced. They existed since Old Testament times, but back then, and up till the 12th century, except for those which belonged to privileged societies, most were smoke holes. King Solomon had bevelled windows. They probably provoked gazing.

In terms of components, windows have graduated – and keep doing so. And like components affect everything else, they affect windows' appearance, function, effectiveness, and durability.

"In the 13th century, window consisted of animal hide, cloth, or wood, and in the 14th and the centuries which followed closely; of flattened pieces of animals' horns, thin pieces of marble, or pieces of glass set in frameworks of wood, iron, or lead. In the Far East, people used paper to fill windows. The Romans introduced glass windows, but it was several eras before they had the transparency that we know today.[6]

In Britain, and later in other parts of Europe, glass windows boosted retail business, when potential customers could see the displays. Today, everyone appreciates glass windows, and for various reasons. There is no comparison with the smoke holes then, and multi-options now, but if we dare to compare; windows today carry a bulk of business' weight. Consultation, and installation, excluding the price of some windows, cost thousands of dollars.

Despite this, equality is not a mark, as was the case with earlier ones. Actually, most windows' only mark then, was functionality. Other features would have been considered superfluity. Like we do with other things, we tend to admire 'nice' windows, but where I'm from, and even in some developing countries two generations ago, this was not a custom. It however, more so, fits the earliest windows in many, if not most Caribbean houses. Many of them were Jalousie. The first one that I recall, and could access by mounting a stool, was a shutter made of wood. Affluence, however avoided – seemed to shun my family – like it did to many others.

There were houses that boasted largeness, thus more rooms, and probably more windows. Others had a window in some rooms. But those the affluent owned, stood apart. Their houses – mansions to us, often boasted two storeys, and at least five rooms, excluding their kitchens. Each room had a window, and they were made of glass.

Do you have a window?

Chapter 2

Rare views

Post Colonial/ Post Slavery Caribbean. Back- track trekking/whirlwind tour. I should have prepared you.

Anyway, meet some characters. First, we will greet affluence.

Sorry. I forgot. I should have warned you. He once associated only with a select few, and if that was reality for a few professionals: people of 'significance', imagine how it was for those who were not.

Yet he has nevertheless, changed, and while not in broader ways, he has, in ways which many appreciate.

That one opposite affluence? She is starkness. Her role? She associated with, and hovered over many of those of 'not much significance.' She also affected the consciences and minds of some of the affluent, and influenced some needed changes.

Affluent peoples' possessions: 'luxuries', awakened intrigue in some have-nots. Glass windows in particular seemed to do that. Children and adults alike, had that disposition. It was contagious. Children more often, seemed to be carriers, but many grown-ups succumbed, and became carriers.

In my hometown, some buildings including a few homes had 'real' windows. Others had 'holes.' Life often surprises us. Things other than coffee get perked. Windows did much perking. At that stage of history in the Caribbean, owning windows – not smoke holes, also birthed status, and glass windows in particular drove the process. It is no wonder many people window gazed.

Some school buildings, like the first two I attended, were open-air structures. The 'Head 'master's or Principal's office, a multi-purpose domain, was for students: enter-only-by-permission, and usually for

3

reprimand. Under lock and key, it also housed records of grades, extra chalks, and text and exercise books including 'free issues.'[7] It also housed a teacher who never spoke a word – yet said much: one whom no student liked, and who must have anticipated the bell at the end of the day, plus weekends, and regular holidays.

Church buildings, Catholic ones especially, featured the most windows, and better yet, stained glass.

Protestant churches had them only in some towns. It seemed all Catholic church buildings had them Some enthusiasts tell us:

"Earlier church buildings narrated biblical characters, and stories, and are packed with action, incident, and grand gestures."[7]

It's no wonder, that despite opposition from some grown-ups from both sides, some of us children of the protestant persuasion, grabbed opportunities to visit our Catholic colleagues' churches.

The windows called us, and that was all I saw. Their stories beckoned and allured us. We became addicts.

Windows do have a language. Some grab attention. It's no wonder that other enthusiasts exult:

"When viewing stained glass windows, vantage points and viewing angles are important."[8]

When we of the Protestant persuasion assembled in our own groups, next to the music, stories, and exhortations, we spent much time gazing at the windows. Their glow mesmerized us, and the novelty did not wane.

Window has other connotations:

"A time period when someone can accomplish something – a critical time – window of opportunity.[9]

There's also window shopping – my favorite. Anyone may shop without hassles – especially no taxes.

Computer's window needs neither introduction nor elaboration. Then, there is also 'window on the world', and everybody has one.

Apart from school, chores at home; including errands, children like me, from families without affluence passed our time driving cars – ones we constructed. What kinds of cars were they?

Intrigue was the car, and it never stalled. Improved living standards for the professionals – a small ripple effect of the industrial revolution, was the engine, and curiosity was the gas. There must have been reasons for the intrigue. There were several, but in retrospect, one stands out. It helped us develop our window on the world.

Everything has singularities. Windows are no exception. They have featured that doors lack, and like stained glass enthusiasts say: they're "action packed." That must be one reason why some travellers excluding me, prefer window seats on planes and trains. I like window seats on trains, but prefer aisle seats on air planes. Does the fact that windows are action-packed, also, at least in part explain why before on- the road entertainment's advent, children vied for window seats in the family car?

Windows have more singularities. For example, whereas doors allow entrance, windows provide viewing and in some cases, enhance safety. In terms of security, it seems that windows have little or none. In some cases, were it not for their sizes, heights, and locations, home invasion through them, would be no problem.

They do, however, have one kind of security that doors do not. If we hear sounds of danger, we investigate the cause through windows, and likely behind curtains; instead of opening doors. Another example of security: no one, especially these days would be even in the back yard, and leave a door open. Yet we can can leave a window or two open while we are out all day.

Like it is with other things, the type of window affects windows' function and durability, but advancement provides movement sensitive, and shatter proof windows. Cost is a deterrent to ownership for many, but for those who can afford it, these features enhance safety and confidence. There is yet one kind of window, used mostly in some business places. This type is like a mirror to those looking from outside. They cannot see what's inside, while those inside can see all that is going on outside.

What is your window?
What story, or stories does it tell?

Chapter 3

Window talks

View is one of window's functions, and like windows, it has various connotations.

"A sight, a look, a systemic survey. An individual and personal perception.[10]

Where I grew up, affluent people's windows enticed viewing. That in turn provoked dreaming, which helped to decrease some of reality's harshness for many who lacked affluence.

Some dreamers could not even imagine ever owning some of the 'luxuries' they glimpsed. Others dreamed on, and still others, like I did, even dared to verbalize it, despite doses of scepticism, and reality orientation:

"Do tell me. Where will your father get money to buy windows and such things? He doesn't even have two extra 'shillings'[11] to jingle in his pockets."

That was a fact, but open for debate. My window on the world, tells me that money is for spending, not for jingling, although some people modeled it like a fashion, when I was a child. It also tells me that God owns everything. He supplies our needs, including glass windows – if He deems it fitting. I wish I knew this back then. This wish, is however, like a horse – one that goes backward, so I will dismount.

Viewing, overall, helped to improve our communication skills, as we argued and debated. While we gaped, we verbalized our systematic perceptions. Even tykes had their say:

"That cost lots of money."

"Yes. Rich people have lots of money. Why don't we have lots of money?"

Big brothers were fountains of knowledge:

"Because we are not rich."

Tykes wanted answers:

"I wish we were rich. Where do rich people get money from?"

Two up from tykes spouted knowledge:

"From the bank."

Tykes' insight always leaked.

"Okay, let's buy some from the bank"

Bigger siblings: under-graduate big brothers, spouted knowledge too:

"Ha, ha. You don't buy money. When you work, they give you money."

Tykes would not settle for less than practicality and action:

"Okay, then I will go to work."

Reality had a voice – 'out of the mouths of babes':

"But at work, you don't get to play."

Some big sisters, had good ideas:

"We could borrow from the bank, but interest would kill us. What we need, is to have relatives or favorite teachers' relatives working there."

Smart Aleks are everywhere. This one shocked some ears:

"Yes, but how did the first people get in there? If you ask me, I'd say we'd have to rob a bank for that kind of money."

"What?!"

Who wanted to see even the threshold of a prison? And, that however, only deterred dreams.

Life had other downsides. "Don't stare." Every child in every culture around the world, has heard this. It was like telling a dog not to bark, but there was one compensation. That rule did not include things.

That's what we thought. O bother, what now?

"Come on. Move along, and keep your eyes before you."

Which is it? Come, or move along? We – I often wondered.

Scolding, and Brusqueness, his cousin, seemed to have steady employment, especially with some people of affluence. Other people of affluence, however, seemed to thrive on the fact that their windows invited ogling. Advantage for them, and for us – more so for us. That was how we saw it. Night-time, with darkness as background, enhanced our viewing. The lights caused the glass to glow, provoking gawking.

Galleries – night galleries. Public viewing – at no cost.

The eyes are our bodies' windows, our hearts are our souls' windows. We are souls with bodies.

Windows have much importance. Sight is a blessing. What we see, leaves lasting impressions. What we say, leaves as much, in fact more, especially on those whose sight malfunctions, and also on children.

People throughout the years, have owned unusual things, but we do not remember those like we do unusual windows: painted over glass windows, for example. There were a few of those in my childhood.

What are some things you saw as a child, that affect you till now?
Why do they affect you?
How do they affect you?

Chapter 4

What's knocking on my window

Regardless of the types, or features, windows have the same purposes. The mere task of imagining life without oxygen, assaults our senses. Lack of light and view? Ignorance, gloom, and listlessness. We can get fresh air and light by going outside, but cannot always do that, so windows bring them to us.

Another of window's uniqueness: open doors allow people into houses, while windows allow fresh air, and probably peeks and glances. We also knock on doors to impart information. One singer invites seekers to "knock on the ceiling"[12,] but it's a rarity to knock on windows, except by prearrangement or in cases of extremity.

That seemed to be the situation, at one point, in my village. There were no phones. It now seems that the lack of that one commodity, allowed people to sleep through the night. These days, in many situations, some people are not able to sleep because of phones. Whatever the case, in those times people slept through the night. "Like a log", some said, but I debate this. Try waking a log.

Anyway, it seemed that often, even two knocks failed to rouse some sleepers. That must have been the reason some people knocked on bedroom windows especially. It meant either severe illness, or death.

More often it was the latter.

Those knocks had three distinctions: loudness, strength, and persistence. It seemed some dogs felt the situation needed their input: "Awoo, awoo, awoooo." either that, or they voiced sympathy.

Whatever the case, a canine choir, without rehearsal, and minus music, was soon in full chorus. The monster, fear, sneaked up, and tried to grab us. No one ever anticipated those knocks. I, for one, dreaded them. Siblings, especially my sister sleeping beside me, provided comfort. Differences and pet peeves were cancelled – for that night at least. Cuddling? Usually it was: "take your knees from my back", but that night, they offered reassurance.

Sensitivity was heightened if it was a child, and more so, if it was a school- mate who'd died. It was with difficulty that we resumed sleep, but often a branch rubbing against a window imitated knock.

Back to dreamland. Thank God. It was only branches, or the person was only ill.

Still another of window's singularities: we can choose not to open doors, but we cannot prevent others from staring at our windows. What and how much they see, depends on whether the window is open, and if it open, it depends on the presence or absence of coverings.

To those inside, windows communicate what is happening outside. During a rainfall, for instance, we can also gauge the rain's strength and progress by a quick glance out a glass window. Gears like raincoats and umbrellas, have outmoded how we view and manage a rainfall, but as a child in the Caribbean, where a rainfall seemed more like a deluge, we had to wait inside till it subsided.

One downside: open windows often allow things we'd prefer to bar. Screens help, but in my childhood only a few had them. There were at least three reasons. Some did not know about them, others did not seem to care, while few could not afford them. The latter was usually the main reason.

Moreover, problems existed even with screens. The openings in some of the earliest ones, allowed crawling insects, and even small birds to enter. Why does anyone, or any animal resist freedom?

Some of those birds flew everywhere else, except the proffered route of freedom. They became fly-in snacks, if there were cats in those houses.

How is your window?
What's getting in?

Chapter 5

Reflections

Our hearts are our outlook on life – our window. Some may not see it immediately, but it's there just like the times when we were children, and discovered windows we didn't know were there.

Hearts provide views: openings for interaction, and thus community. We broadcast our outlook through our words and behavior, although more so, through our words. And just like light causes glass to glow in the dark, we who know God, reflect Him, and draw others to Him. People wonder at our glow. It may begin with curiosity and investigation, with room for disputes, and suspicion, just like open windows may attract other than our reasons for opening them.

Varieties of windows abound, likewise, personalities, thus the varied outlooks on life. All windows despite type or cost, have the same purpose, so despite personalities, and stations, we provide interaction: material for community. Variety adds much to life. Our varied outlooks can enrich others.

We just need awareness, sensitivity and care.

Open windows provide views. Some people seem tempted and satisfied to peek through cracks, but we get better pictures via open windows. To those inside, they communicate what's outside, and vice versa. A window cannot prevent people from looking, peeking, or investigating. No more can we prevent others from looking at us, and making assumptions. It is a two-way exchange. We do the same, and it is ongoing. Some assumptions are close to correct. Others need correction. The type of window affects how it works.

Fixed windows speak for themselves. They are not for opening. They allow light, but not much ventilation. Am I like this, limiting viewing?

Privacy and suspicion are guards. Which is preferred, a little light, but no ventilation, or ventilation, but no light?

Storm windows withstand any weather. They reduce the flow of air, thus promoting energy sufficiency.

We all know people with that disposition. They portray strength. Nothing uproots them. Circumstances may rattle them, but they face them with strength, even when there is friction.

Picture windows have width, which promotes light, and enhances viewing. People with picture window personalities, have a transparency that attracts, and invites and promotes interaction. Our lives can be like picture windows, because God's love permeates us.

Skylight windows are on the ceiling, acting like overhead fixtures. It seems like they are trying to grasp the sun. They too, promote energy sufficiency. People like this, just glow.

Stained glass windows defy description, they speak through enthusiasts:

"The message of our medium is light, translucency, radiancy, refraction, reflection, brilliancy spark, illumination, inspiration."[13]

It may seem an impossibility, but we can be skylights, and stained-glass windows.

Sliding windows open with ease, allowing ventilation. All windows allow ventilation, but this type excels. I have a debt of gratitude for people with flexibility. They have, over the years, taught me open and vent – with caution.

There are windows that stand ajar. Doors that fit this description, speak of invitation and access, but with limits. Windows that stands ajar, however, send a different message. Reasons, including intention may have caused that position. Maybe the handle is broken, thus it is stuck. This angle can alter or distort view. Those looking in, may see nothing, or may see things only in part, just like the owner intends.

Other windows are bolted in tightness. I recall some. Theories and assumptions for their closures abounded. Some of us wouldn't get close, and less so, peek in, while for others, curiosity was an itch that defied avoidance.

Painted glass windows stand out the most, in my memory. They seemed like contradictions. Owners had reasons, but they failed to realize that caused itching. Was the paint a type of screen, and if it was, what was it screening? A few owners, after renovation, re-opened painted closed windows.

Some new owners brought changes, but if affluence befriended former owners, they cured the itch, and also introduced welcome changes.

Screens bar some things, including those which cause no harm. Just like we put in window screens, we screen our hearts. And like screens limit the amount of light, so without awareness, we may block needed interaction. Glass windows, used for promoting sales, also enticed intrusion, especially in shops.

Viewers needed to see displays, but some viewers were thieves. That must have been a predicament until burglar bars provided a solution.

As believers, we're like glass windows, although situations may cause temporary opaqueness. We want openness, but we fear *other things* may get in. We desire interaction, yet bar intrusion.

Which type of window describes your heart at the moment?
Is it in need of repair?

Chapter 6

Who used my window?

Like they do with other things, some people misuse windows. Reality justifies the fact: type affects function. The object, however, as in the case with windows, is not the problem. Rather, it is the unorthodox uses.

Disdain barged in when she opened her window. She did not bar it.

Just look at him. If I did not know it, no one could convince me that he's king. My father had much against him, but despite all, he had more dignity. I probably need to teach my husband how to behave like a king. She could not wait to begin the lessons.

"What demonstration of dignity. What honorable behavior. The king uncovered himself – for *all* to see."[14]

Fizzzz.

He did not expect it. Neither did he appreciate, need, or want it. Fatigue, zeal, and gladness tussled in every muscle. Zeal refused to relent. He'd initiated dancing in the street, and nothing could make him regret what he'd done. Praise to Yahweh! His heart kept dancing.

Now to attend to what he thought, but hoped he had not heard. Did she say what she did? He must get his message across?

"I danced to express my delight in Yahweh. The one who gave us victory – the same one who chose me above your father. I will celebrate, despite your feelings!"[15]

King David probably realized later that one cannot recall an arrow, once it leaves the sling.

I should have toned it down – seasoned it with graciousness. But why can she not see? My reason for dancing should have provoked her to join me! It's not the object. It's the significance.

For Yahweh's sake, the ark is back among us!

We do likewise today: gaze in secret – use our *windows*: mock and gossip. We throw arrows without thinking about the effect. Looking at others from windows, however, needs not be negativity. When I was a girl, many grownups watched children from windows. What a surprise, and sometimes shame, when they confronted us about some behaviors. Our awareness of that practice curbed many unacceptable behaviors, albeit, the motive stemmed from fear of consequences.

People watching us from windows can help in other ways. In my early childhood, telephones were a a rarity. Children were like telephones, relaying *select* messages between families, relatives, and neighbors. We enjoyed those jobs, and as well, adventures. Some bordered on risks.

In retrospect, it was a blessing to have *mothers and fathers,* everywhere it seemed.

"Where are you going?"

"Mama sent me …"

"Okay. Come here to me, if you need water, or anything."

"Yes, mam", or, sir."

Sometimes, our response was:

"Papa …said."

Retrace, your steps. Go home, right now!

Index fingers in action, spoke with eloquence and authority. Any hint of suspicion seemed to ignite curiosity, and fanned protection. Parents would not send us into danger. How did those standby parents know when we lied? And how many dangers did their interventions avert?

I learned to behave according to grownup's expectations. Someone was likely watching from a window, or more. It however, had dividends which I grasped, only nearly a lifetime later. Many of those who watched and confronted us, had reasons. They probably had the same experiences, so wanted to protect us. At the stage in our youth, where we did not fully grasp God's word; fear made an inroad. I speak mostly for myself.

At one point, the fear of ghosts topped the list, that, and fear of the strap. The strap was often a necessity. Both, though more so, the strap, helped to reinforce obedience, and other virtues in many from my generation. On the subject of ghosts: who in his/her right mind wished to meet one? They were predictable, but still …

Ghosts: "duppies" in the local vernacular, was a subject: a window by itself – and a mystery. For instance: why did they like darkness, fear whistling, rise at midnight, select people to strike, and disappear at the first hint of dawn? Sealed lips reveal much. They also instigate, and as well, provoke. What was it that provoked curiosity: 'inquisitiveness' then, and still provoke now?

Just like they disappeared before dawn, so did the belief in them, with maturity. Yet, that fear was a reinforcement. Meanwhile, I maintained some of the itch. I wondered what they looked like, and hoped I would even glimpse one. It seemed, however, that they either didn't know my address, feared me, or busyness kept them at other houses.

While I stood by windows, peeking, other windows gained clarity as some darkness began to dissipate. I recalled how much the skies resembled dark blue bedspreads, with thousands of lights pinned on. I mused on the fact that God made everything, including people. I thought of Sunday school teachers' words that God loves everyone. I wavered between doubt and belief that God loved me. It felt like many people did not like me, so it excited me to dare believe that God loved me as an individual.

While I stood there, other windows began to open.

I am not scared of ghosts like I used to be, I internalized one time.

Some people must have noticed, because some opened new windows for me:

"She's not much of a scared cat, like she used to be", one window opener opined.

I used my new window, albeit, without words.

I'm not a scared cat!

"Girl, fix your face: quit scowling." The window opener refused to close her window.

I have fixed my face the way I want it. I will not look through your window.

Others misused windows in other ways.

"Mrs. D., Mrs. D, did you notice any strangers in the yard this morning?" the speaker asked with mounting excitement.

"No. Is something wrong?" The neighbor's eyes spoke volumes.

"Come and look, Mrs. D."

"I can't believe a thief came while I was weeding in the front, all morning", the neighbor's tone dripped with disappointment and disgust.

"Ah Mrs. D. He took the profit from the sale of the cow." The upturned mattress was the hint.

"He must have entered through the back window. Too late for you now, still we must board up all back windows. They entice thieves", the neighbor was pleased to have a solution.

Mrs. D's watchfulness, and empathy helped much. Each home owner was a watchman for the other. One neighbor's loss was loss to another. That was another type of window.

What kind of illegal entries have others made through your window?

Chapter 7

Entrances

Often, the window's type, size, and location made a difference. Thieves intruded most frequently through wooden shutters, and through large, rear windows, on ground level. Lovers such as Romeo used windows for wooing at nights, and through the centuries, others used them for the same reason. Some young people in the town where I lived, used them to escape to place of prohibition. This occurred not only in homes, but also in boarding schools, more so, in boarding schools. In some homes, older brothers headed this list.

The prohibition, despite consequences of spurning, it seemed only a suggestion. Furthermore, there were ways to get around consequences— or so, spurners thought. Why not put promises to use? After all, boons captivate benefactors.

"Stan, I heard that the show makes the hair on the skin stand up."

"Comes what may Cal, I shall see it. What about you?"

"What a question to pose. Like you, I shall see it!"

"A concern, however, Stan voiced. "Older sisters, even though they're only three years older?

Stand- in mothers. Too bossy for my liking."

He lacked no uncertainty. Calvin, his friend grew a few centimeters in front of his eyes.

"I don't have that problem, Stan. I'm the oldest, so next to papa, and mama; I'm boss. My problem is my little sister. Man alive, she comes close to fitting James's talk about the tongue."

He'd heard the same talk about the wrong use of the tongue, but couldn't agree with Calvin.

"That's stretching it a bit for a little girl, Cal, but I see what you mean. Girls yak too much.

Yet there must be a way. My sisters would love to go dancing, but mama, and papa veto it.

I'm middle child. And a son! I can attend dances. I could be my sister's passport. We can forge a deal."

It was a must for both friends. Nothing, or no one must stand in the way.

"I am all for the bargaining", Calvin offered. "Younger brothers can be a pain, but if you can help them, or offer something they like; they can be puppets or putty."

"Either works well, although putty creates a mess. Speaking of either. Cal, here comes your little brother."

"Puppet! And the strings work well. Imagine us seated and watching the show, Stan."

"Deal Cal. I must hurry, lest stand- in mama quizzes me. I cannot afford to be on bad terms with her now."

Opportunity came walking. Calvin could not let it pass by.

"So, Charles, Gulliver Salmon."

"Yes, brother Calvin."

"I heard you did well in some kind of contest. That's good. School's, okay? How's arithmetic these days? Acing it? Your 'catapult'[16] needs disrepair, or would you prefer a new one? And what about your gig?[17]

Wrestling match. Cloud versus sunshine. Cloud is on the mat: Charles's face. One …ten. And the champion is sunshine!

Cloud is trying to make a come-back. Get him sunshine.

"No brother Calvin. I'm not acing it, but would like to. I got C plus ……"

"C plus? My brother got C in arithmetic?" Calvin was aware of his voice pitch.

"Teacher said I passed, but only by a hairbreadth. What is a hairbreadth?"

"Forget about hairbreadth, Charlie. Anything less than B plus, is failure – for a Salmon."

"I really want to ace all again. And I would like a new Catapult, and a Gig."

"You can have it all Charlie. I can help you, but I'd like your help with a little matter."

Who was the artist, translating wonder on his little brother's face? And had Charlie only imagined what thought he heard? Was his almost- a man brother, who was going to be a teacher, going to help, but even better, asking for his help?

"Okay, brother Calvin. How can, I mean, how may I help you?"

"Either term is okay. You have the ability, and I am giving you permission."

Someone kept turning up the sun. For the third time, Charlie had failed to tie for first place with his pal, Herman, but he just knew he would again. Brother Calvin, of all people was offering his help.

"Okay, little brother. You are not little any more. Anyhow, here is how you can help me.

There's a show, and I am going to see it."

Was it shock, doubt, or fear for brother Calvin, or was it secret admiration? The latter won. Surely brother Calvin was not going to dis …. well not listen to papa and mama? Furthermore, 'a Christian does not attend movies.'

He knew where he was, but someone else acted his role, while he looked on, that evening.

"Charlie. Are you not feeling well?"

"No. I mean yes … I am 'hearty'[18,] mama."

"Well then, finish your dinner. You're dreaming with your eyes open. It is too early for that. With this strange interference in God's ordained time, it seems to get dark earlier. Soon it will be dark."

Calvin longed to discuss daylight saving time, yet he must change the subject.

"Right Charlie. And by the way, I heard that goats untether themselves, get home, and even settle themselves for the night."

Ho, ho, ho.

Something in that, leaned hard on Charlie's humor. No wonder he liked his big brother. He could turn frowns upside down. Mrs. Salmon too appreciated her eldest's input. Nevertheless, from whom did he inherit that kind of talk? Which side of the family? Not bad, but still ….

Mean while A minus, B plus, news about shows, Gigs and Catapults battled for dominance. Gigs and catapults claimed dominance – after A scores. All was well with life. He must tell Mille all that brother Calvin said about shows. She would maybe get scared, but anyway.

"Millie, brother Calvin is going to …….." he'd hazarded.

He'd gone close to the brink, almost over it.

"Just between us men, Charlie. Girls yak too much. That can be a danger especially now. One word at the wrong time, bye, bye opportunity to see the show."

What a save – that recall, and just in time. Miss out on hearing about heroes like 'The One Armed Armed Sword Guy?'[19] That must not – would not happen. And he must help Brother Calvin re-enter by the same route and method.

What was that? Was it crackling, or cracking? Sounded like something … breaking. And it seemed to happen every time there was a new one in town. What was it?

Were you ever someone's puppet?

Chapter 8

Whispering at the window

Movie night. It was not because he did not try. Despite the solemnity of any vow, and regardless of anticipation, somnolence overrides- wins. Calvin and Stanley were in another world after. The hero stowed away with Calvin.

"Stan. Did your hair stand straight when the guy drew his sword? Mine did."

"Yes. Cold sweat was close. And what a scream from whom else, but a girl? Confirms my feeling: the movies' no place for girls."

Two other attendees went with them that night. They always attend – incognito. Number one loves movies. Many movie goers love and prefer him. He's fun, and he's all for positivity. The other? He's a fun choker. Many disregard him. He does not mind anyway. He knows satisfaction when anyone shows interest in his ways.

Number one chooses Stanley as he and Calvin part company. He notices that the moon and stars are taking a break. They were on duty earlier. He hopes Stanley has not noticed, but introduces banter, a pal. To Stanley, the sky seems like an all-out strike. No problem anyway. Folks say 'they' fear whistling', so here goes. News about whistling in the dark circulated later. His company beamed.

Stanley was good company – a believer. Time to help Calvin.

He already has company, however. Of course, the fun choker. Why does he even bother to stick around? Not many, if any at all, like or want his company. Anyway, he would sway Calvin, like he had done to Stanley.

Meanwhile, Calvin relived it all, as he neared his house. Certainty buoyed him. Charlie would drink it all in, and more so, as he Cavin rehashed it with precision and details, but he would wait for day time, when they were alone.

Pull, pull.

"It's wet. I do not recall it rai …. Charlie, Charlie."

If he put his mouth any closer, he would bite the window.

"Charlie, Charlie", he tried again.

He could not yell any softer. He may as well talk to the window. He would probably get a better response.

It seems there was no alternative. The 'fun choker' wanted to help Calvin, and it seems to be working. Calvin concluded he'd better knock, after all. The 'fun choker's head seemed to know only one direction. It seemed he could not move his head from side to side.

Nah. I would not if I were you. Number one would not be outdone.

Calvin felt optimism seep out. Frustration and annoyance waltzed in.

"The little traitor He probably broke down and told Millie, who tattled to mama and papa.

But still he could have found a way."

Just do it. There's no pleasantness, but it has dividends. The fun choker stayed with him.

His role was right on, but there was no time for more reflection. Someone came to the door.

"Calvin, I did not hear you go out. Why did you lock the door? Where is the key? Why didn't you take the lamp?"

Something was going on. The strange talk earlier, and now …

"Why on earth did you get dressed to go to the outhouse, Calvin, Christopher Salmon?"

Oh no, Calvin thought. Word war. There'd be one winner. It would not be him. Why did all the well-rehearsed, just- in case ammunition defect? On second thought, however, what providence that it was not papa who came to the door. Mama's bark had toughness, and without effort, she always won hands-down. He would, however, recover. Papa skipped the bark on such occasions. His bites? That's a story by itself.

How do you use your window?

Do you need help opening it sometimes?

Chapter 9

Ins and outs

Calvin like dancing. He was dancing – on the inside. This new one was another hit, he'd heard.

"Millie."

"What."

That did not sound like his little sister. Nevertheless, he must exercise caution, even while maintaining decorum, and a big brother's place.

"Millie!"

"Coming, brother Calvin."

That was more like it.

"Look what I got just for you. Isn't it the biggest, juiciest ….?"

"Thanks, brother Calvin!"

His little sister was ready for the bounty. He was ready to grab the new one too, but he must exercise caution, and calmness.

"Not so fast. You already cleaned your teeth. Wait till morning. I will guard it for you.

Besides, it is nearly dark, and you know who comes at night, and what they do."

"Okay brother Calvin. I will go to bed now."

One down – the one who could cause difficulties. One to go. Yet he needed caution, even while hiding it. He knew he would manage.

"Charlie, mama and papa are on cloud nine, and I need not guess the reason."

"I am glad, brother Calvin. Thanks for the help with my sums. I came close to tying with Herman. I got a B plus this time. Teacher said I need to buckle up on Geometry."

"That's more like it. You're climbing. Aim for A we'll work on it", Calvin encouraged.

"Okay, and thanks too for the sling. Now I can get big juicy mangoes for mama and Millie.

I did not win the Gig contest, but maybe next time. Please, brother Calvin, I promise to stay awake next time, and like you, I want to become a teacher, maybe a math teacher."

What was that fragrance? Who was wearing it? There was just something about it. Was something happening?

Boys stole out the window to attend movies, girls; to attend dances. The ball seemed to in be the older sister's court. If she had no older brother, she must rely on younger sisters. That often came with a price.

Mel had to at least say something. If her little sister continued like that, there'd not be enough sugar left to make the cake to share at school. It was for the sake of her sister's health too.

"Norma, that's stealing. Furthermore, you'll soon lose all your teeth. Stop sticking out your tongue at me. That's not showing respect. I am older than you."

Was it language barrier or disregard? Mel must however maintain her place. She was aware of, and did not like the new war. She could not allow that behavior go on. Her sister too, seemed ready to battle.

"Stop it. I did not realize I had a lizard for a sister. You look like one now", Mel continued.

"I am not stealing, and I don't have a lizard's tongue. Your thighs are big as a cow's, and you are not my boss!"

Mel could not believe it was the same little sister she thought was all sweetness. She wasn't, at the moment. She felt she could disown her, without any qualms.

Weighed, however: the crave to attend the dance, lust for revenge, and the fairness in the demand for respect. Latter two outweighed. Mel imagined herself in an abandoned building, with the nearest person two houses away. There, she would scream for five minutes.

Mama and papa must not hear about her plan, and neither must Nellie, especially not Nellie.

Baby sisters, till they change, are sweetness itself, except for their tattling, Mel's frustration grew.

They do it all in innocence, I realize. Was I like that? No, I am the oldest. Aagh.

One – actually two advantages, however revved her spirit. Younger sisters, especially next in age, make great confidants. They also believe they profit more in most bargains. Time to hone in.

"Norma", Mel rallied as they washed dishes later. Mama and others say I'm almost as tall as papa",

and you're closing in on me."

"My goodness, Mel, it's true. I'm almost up to your shoulders." The bait was heat to Norma's wax: sullenness.

"Must you prove everything, Norma? Anyway, my best Sunday skirt that Aunt Bea sent from England is too short for modesty. I could lengthen …."

The wax was melting with speed.

"Oh please, Mel. I will hem …. I mean, I will take it. I will do anything for that skirt."

Hmm. She said, anything. Dance, here I come! Mel felt like dancing.

"No need to beg for it, Norma. We are sisters, after all. Another matter. You will soon be a high school miss, and papa will permit you to perm your hair. I will do it for you."

"Thanks Mel. I like the way you do your hair. Please do mine, the same way."

"Okay, Norma. I can practice when papa is not around, but I need a teeny favour."

"Just name it, Mel!"

It seemed Norma was listening to inner music, and liked dancing like Mel did. That could be big help. She must maintain the heat.

"I want to attend a birthday dance for a friend – an all-girls dance. Just try to keep it from Nellie."

"Mel!" Norma could not believe it. "Anyway", she added with haste," Good thing, I'm her…. favourite sister, sorry Mel."

"Oh well. And please, mama must not know about it either", Mel cautioned.

"You know mama. She misses nothing", Norma's brows appeared like one line.

"Find some way to distract her while I go through the window."

"Another problem Mel, Norma added." Gyp loves you and follows you around. How will I prevent her from following you and barking?"

"The skirt's waiting, so is the hairstyle, which you may be the first to model, Norma."

Suspense, like a flammable liquid, saturated these incidents, if it threatened to rain. Parents in innocence, closed windows: doors for the occasion, and often discovered that sons were missing. Those deviators must then sleep in cellars: Caribbean type basements. Didn't ghosts hang out there? And something even worse hung out there too. Ghosts could do horrible things, but at least a victim could predict their behavior. If deviators had a choice, they would probably have chosen ghosts. But why?

What changed tail -wagging friends, into growling fiends? It seemed that those *new mothers/* snarling fiends made a statement: "We must agree with the visits to see our babies." For what other purpose was the human friend visiting their temporary domain that time of the night? The deviators hated trying to back out in a stooped position. Most of those spaces did not even accommodate a child's height. It was also a task trying to maintain eye contact with the mother, but it was a necessity.

It was either that, or re-enter the house by the right route, and face the music – one usually in sharp tones. Some deviators took note. Others didn't. Were they tone deaf?

It was a rarity that girls got locked out. What were big brothers for? Besides, everyone needs a a favour sometimes.

"Aldyth, I need my blue shirt for Friday night. Would you please rinse it?" Steve ordered.

"Of course, I can rinse a shirt. The question is, do I want to? Another question. Do you want me to just rinse it, or do you want me to wash it first? I recommend that. And I bet you would also like me to run over it with an iron." Aldyth sensed her brother was up to something.

"Must you always pick sense out of nonsense? Steve honed in. Anyway, since you force me, I will tell you. There's a movie I must see."

"Well, Mr. favored. You at least get to attend something. Girls get veto for everything."

It was time for the bait.

"There's also a dance coming up at the club! Our own local band will be playing."

"When will that be?!" The fish bit.

"In two weeks. Look. You like to dance like I do. I love movies. So, let's help each other. I will butter up mama, and she can work on papa. I will promise her to watch you at the dance."

"Why do you need to watch me? What do they think happens at dances, except moving to the beat? Mama moves well to music at church. Anyway, bring the shirt. I will wash and iron it. And I will try to cover you when you go to the movies." The fish was not about to get out of the bait.

Other related behaviors mystified – bothered many minds.

"I tell you with certainty. It is the work of a small child, most likely a boy. The space is too small for a teenager or adult", the father of a '*suspect*' opined.

"I cross-questioned my boys with a whip in hand, still they denied it. Other parents have done the same, with similar response, and came to the same conclusion."

"I'm convinced too, they didn't. The question, however, remains: who did it?"

The mystery soon unravelled. A family reported coming home and finding a small boy, with dried tears, asleep in their living room. The boy said "the man" put him through the window. A child was the accomplice. An unwilling accomplice. How much of this behavior occurred? And with what frequency?

Has anyone ever forced you through his/her window?

Chapter 10

I borrowed your window

I was not above misusing windows. Come with me on a trip – another one – across the years. Here we are. I was the first one home from school that afternoon. It was too early to do my homework. It was math, and I not like math. I had to do something to occupy my mind. Eaves drop on my conversation with myself, as I looked around, then focused on an old neighbor.

Her widow is open. Her bed is right under it. She is resting, probably dozing. That piece of bark will do it. Someone tore it from a tree in his/her Tarzan imitation. We also used it as a skipping rope. The rains puffed it up, the sun dried it out again. Now it looks like a …..... snake.

She dreads them like I do. It will land beside her, or on her, and she will scream – like I did the first time a boy chased me with a real one. Teacher says their venom lacks poison, but I still do not trust them.

It was all quietness in the big yard. Only Rover one of our dogs, seemed to be around. She was busy wagging her tail, and sniffing. I was sure no one would know who did it. Everyone knew I raid the fruit orchard after school. Only one little matter, however, could grow, if I dwelt too much on it. It floored me. How did someone like her, with a vision challenge, able to identify ….

Anyway, if it got to that, everyone would defend me. They knew I would not even glance at the pictures of reptiles. I knew that could cause me to fail science. Anyway. I let Rover go with me to the orchard. I like dogs for many reasons. I especially like the way they smack their lips sometimes.

I now agree there are no excuses for misconduct, but I was only halfway between fourteen and fifteen.

My window needed both cleaning and adjustment – mostly cleaning. A passerby reported hearing screams. She alerted neighbors. Investigation revealed a piece of bark on an elderly neighbor woman's bed. There were no witnesses, but some suspect a fourteen-plus neighbor girl. The case is, however in suspense. The alibi is within reason. Mrs. Sharpe, the District Attorney, and the plaintiffs' niece, feels that guilt riddles the defendant. She concludes that while the plaintiff's eyesight malfunctions; the suspect's insight malfunctions, but time and maturity will soften the conscience, and improve the insight.

Coincidence? Evidence? Some believed there was a link. An elderly male neighbor noted "she worked hard that that evening." A former Sunday school remarked: "She weeds with skill, like her mother."

The suspect's own mother stated: "Zeal overcame knowledge. Some tomato plants disappeared with the weeds."

I misused windows in other ways. Another time, anger, avidness, and smugness buoyed and landed me at my destination. I lacked no certainty that the Sunday school teacher would defend me.

"She …… and she said that …………..." It was good to unload my indignation.

"I'm getting only your side of the story. I need hear her side too," my should-have been defender responded with calmness.

"But she ………" I pushed.

"Like I said. It is one sided. Why don't you go back and talk it over with her? If you still feel cheated, invite her to come and talk it over, together with me."

She does not believe me, she does not like me, I concluded.

The afternoon became like night. I had much to learn. I'd opened a window which posed dangers I could not see. That grownup friend forced me close it, although it was several years later that I understood.

How do you use your window?

Chapter 11

Mud on the windows

Even with the correct use, our first window took much beating. My siblings and I, more so I, liked to play with the handle. No scolding daunted our pleasure. As sunset casts shadows on the slanted slats, I discovered I could make my own 'movies' as I twisted and turned the handle. My siblings did the same. Sometimes we did it together. Even the times my parents used it the correct way, added to, and hastened its demise. It finally came of in my hand. I would miss my shows. I couldn't understand why it upset my mother when she could not close the window. Would she miss the shows too?

Also, in houses like ours, where owners couldn't afford glass windows; darkness prevailed. During rainfalls: cloudbursts, we either closed them, and endured the stuffiness and gloom, or opened them to light, but let the rain enter and create problems. There were already other leaks, so we did not need more stress. I disliked the stuffiness, but disliked the gloom more, especially as I approached middle childhood.

I liked running through the rain sometimes, but did not like it coming through the window. I anticipated the relief when someone could open the window to air and light.

Some in my grandparent's generation, had beliefs which must have held plausibility for them.

"The air is not good for the sick. Close the window, lest he/she gets worse."

That seemed to be law until …

"Okay, Doctor. Maybe just a …..."

Even the sick recognized boundaries:

"Don't argue with the Doctor. Throw the window open."

"Right", the Doctor agreed. "We can never get too much air."

"Okay, Doctor", all agreed.

Had they timed it? Was it an unwritten agreement? A game? Doctor's departure. Belief reinstated. Now I I know the main reason I liked the Doctor's visits.

It seemed also, that some did not understand window's role in emergencies. In the Caribbean, many families' kitchens were separate from the houses. Those families prepared their meals over open fires in the open- air kitchens. One, elderly neighbor, however, prepared hers indoors on her kerosene oil stove. A few times when she released too much of the fluid, a small fire erupted. Over time, it became a predictability. It seemed no one could convince her that when she cooked, it was better to leave the window open.

Slam!

"Mrs. Makki just slammed her window shut. Something's up", a neighbor voiced her concern.

The person who'd rescued her the first time that occurred, and rushed to help, remembered:

"Fire. Somebody, anybody, help."

Creak. Crank. Fizz. Cough. Push. Ah.

That time, her next-door neighbor/tenant rescued her by thrusting the window open, turning off the stove and smothering the flame. The fresh air diffused the acridity, and saved the day.

Closed windows can also guard against the elements, but sometimes, however, they are no match against them. Hurricanes often batter the Caribbean. In my childhood, we faced them with fear and fascination. The wind in aggression, screamed and bullied for obeisance. A few trees complied, but at least maintained their roots. Windows, especially some without firm grounding, tried to fly off their hinges, either in fear or counter aggression. Fathers, or big brothers often had to insert ten-penny nails[20] for fortification, or put in new windows after the onslaught.

Later, when I resided in West Africa, I dreaded something similar: Harmattan: the dry and dusty season.

During Harmattan, the wind picks up, and swirls dust, and even with windows closed, the dust gets into houses, forcing owners to cover everything with sheets, or dust every day, and in some cases, several times per day. It leaves with reluctance and vengeance once the rainy season begins.

My first encounter presented a situation which I hated and dreaded. I also started to understand and appreciate windows a little more. After I started to learn, ensuring that all windows were closed before I headed out, even for a few hours, became a priority on my checklist. It is a major part of my memories.

"What happened?" I could not believe what I was seeing.

"Sorry. I noticed you left your windows open, and wished I had a way to close them for you."

I was not aware I'd lamented out loud, till my next-door neighbor approached in calmness, and anyway, I was past caring who heard me. She introduced a new window. One I needed at the moment, and would need again, and again. My heart seemed to have shifted focus. I had no desire or intention for it. I did not like it. Everything around me seemed to be mud, or going to mud.

"Even when the sky is blue, and the heat is like a furnace - like they always are; still close your windows, before you go out."

I wished I'd paid more attention. I'd heard that before.

"It will be like playing with mud. Where do I begin?" What I was seeing, happened only in nightmares.

"'Sai hankuri', most missionaries including me, learn the hard way. Welcome aboard, to missionary life." She attempted reassurance.

I appreciated her consolation, including help with the language I was learning. With all my heart, I wanted to 'wear patience', but surely, I did not have to, in that situation. It seemed the clean-up would take longer than forever. After just a few minutes into clean-up, I did not recognise my fingernails. I opened a new window. Self pity and a bit of anger slipped in, and hid from everyone. They came out only when I was alone, at bedtime especially. I wanted the weather, especially Harmattan, to adapt to me. It was not about to — at any time.

My physical windows lacked effectiveness because I'd failed to use them like I should. My new window did not help. What a difference it made, when I learned. Soon, I preferred coming home to stuffiness, and a little dusting, rather than to coolness and the frustration of battling with mud, and trying to rescue possessions such as books from Harmattan's claim.

Harmattan could not behave otherwise. Once it senses rain's initial appearance for the season, it seems to retaliate. Its wind lifts dust and everything that it can, high in the air. Even daylight seems to hide.

Small black plastic bags contribute much to the appearance of darkness. As the wind swirls the dust and bags around, daylight is obscured. Often, mid mornings look like late evening, and early afternoons; like night time. Usually with the first hint, the 'wise', with varied speed, cover everything; securing the corners with weighty objects, then seeks shelter.

I was not using the shelter available to all. I could not handle it, and often wished I was anywhere else. I concluded I was not missionary material. I am no Amy Carmichael, I thought. It seemed Harmattan blew away my joy in serving Jesus. There must be some solution.

'Eureka'. Some people have remarked that I wear my heart on my face. The way I am feeling now, leaders may conclude I don't meet the criteria for missionary perseverance.

Visions of going home: comfort zones flirted. Often, I envisioned myself back home without any qualms. The physical windows put up a good fight, most of the times, but my other window malfunctioned despite its coverings.

Circumstances can batter, and even alter, but need not condition our outlook. We cannot avoid some situations. Expecting them, just like as missionaries, we knew the first rain of the season could happen anytime, during Harmattan, helps much. We may feel kike quitting, like I did after my first encounter. But just like the experienced missionaries' input helped me, so others' input can help. We can help each other, if we are open to it. It is like learning to live with, and handle new windows.

How is your window?
Is it open, or do you keep it closed?

Chapter 12

Insights on outlooks

Windows in high locations – upstairs windows, enhance viewing things in a distance, and at a lower level. They can, however, equally distort them. Depending on the objects, some may appear smaller than they are. Even large things can appear small. Sometimes also, those viewers see more than they should.

When I was a girl, some people of affluence viewed their non-affluent neighbors from their vantage points. Some disdained what they saw, others viewed with neutrality, and some took matters in their own hands.

"Quite a brood you have there, Mr. Stern. It boggles my imagination, how you house, clothe, and feed them. I could take one off your hand.'

I was within hearing range. I did not grasp it all, but recall a window my father opened:

"My children are not puppies. You may have a free puppy, when our dog whelps, any day now."

I glanced through the window she opened.

Does she want to be our mother? Can someone have two mothers? It would be nice: gas stove, better yet, many glass windows.

I moved away from that window, with haste. I was glad I belonged to my family.

How she gathered information, puzzled me for a while, then naivety departed. While she sat relaxing by window, she watched us. She meant no harm, but tact and correctness were either hiding, or had defected.

Another viewer, better- off- than- my family, but minus the affluence, also lived on a hill.

"I can touch the glass window."

One of the girls we knew from the school playground, crowed as a friend and I went by their house.

"So what? I can too. Stop showing off."

Her brother was a hero – for the moment. My righteousness was far below the Pharisees'. Gloating was a tidbit I wanted to savor for a while.

Windows in the opposite position, can also distort view. Objects can appear larger than they are, because of the viewer's angle and viewpoint. Some non-affluent viewers approached life from their vantage points too.

"Life is so unfair", one neighbor unloaded to another. "I heard that the 'Affluents', two houses up the hill, have meat at every meal, while some of us have it only two times per week."

"Even if it's true, why hold it against them?", the listener chastised. "They cook outside like the rest of us, and their college son carries groceries on his head, like many of us do", the listener concluded.

We all have windows, and whether we like it, or not, others view them, like we viewed the contents in peoples' houses through their windows at night. Windows are two ways: we look outside at others, and they look in at us. From their vantage points, those on 'hills' look down, and vice versa, those in 'valleys' fail to realize that appearances lack accuracy.

How is your view?
What is your vantage point?
Does it need adjustment?

Chapter 13

Dream Windows, Breaks, and Patches

It seemed some people derived happiness from owning windows. Then there were those who derived their happiness from discussing those people's windows. Despite seeming contentment, many yearned for something better. Glass windows was a dream, although for many, it remained at the dream stage.

Owning them, however, required certain responsibilities. That seemed to breed sensitivity, caution, stress, and tension in some. The foremost problem with glass windows in those days, was that before long, someone either cracked or broke them. Reactions depended on employers' or parents' moods or personalities.

"Do be careful, Dottie. You do a good job. Don't let carelessness with the windows spoil it."

"Okay, thanks Miss."

In other places:

"Your clumsiness will cost you, Winnie. Don't expect full pay till we replace the window!"

"Sorry Miss."

"Neither tears, nor words will help, so turn them off, please."

In some households:

"Money does not grow on trees. Your poor father works his fingers to the bones to provide decency for the family. You have ruined it all."

"I did not do it on purpose, mama."

As children, we certainly caused much frustration. We broke wooden window handles, and later glass windows, through misuse and accident. In retrospect, while I do not agree with the overreactions, I now understand the frustration. Some of the affluent, more so the less affluent, could not afford to replace them, so they either ignored the cracks, or patched them. That was a trigger for word war.

Like children all over the world, we in the Caribbean had spats with frequency. Some from households blessed with affluence, were almost, always the aggressors/instigators.

They knew how to use ammunition with effectiveness:

"Just because you got B plus, you think you're great. Well, you're not, Miss patched/wooden window."

That never failed to poke my sensitivity.

Often, some of the shamed, including me, succumbed.

"Everyone else has glass windows. Why do we have wooden ones?" I whined.

"Everyone else? Most of us have wooden windows. As long as it works, it does not matter what type it is."

My mother attempted to correct my outlook. It, however, took years for me to grasp that fact, plus the reality that those of us from homes with wooden or patched windows, outnumbered those with perfect ones.

A few facts about windows, defied avoidance and denial. Wooden windows lacked their counterpart's popularity. For example, they never invited a second look, yet they had their strengths. They did not break with the same ease, so didn't require the same caution in handling. Also, along with their tendency to break, glass windows amassed spots. Fingers created smears on the inside, while dust, rain, dead insects, and dried leaves created smudges on the outside.

Even dreams, ambition, and fun got implicated over glass windows. I wonder now if some people who had glass windows hated ball games, or did their enjoyment of the game cause some of them to overlook cracks and breakages? Many people enjoyed Cricket. A park was available for it, and anyone could play there, anytime. But when the urge called, any spot seemed okay in the minds of some enthusiasts.

Who wants to play ball?

What a question to ask young male enthusiasts, dreaming about their heroes, or imagining they were the hero.

Stance. Dream. Aim.

Cr... ack.

Oh no. Run home. Sorry you did not get to do the home run.

Some innocent amateurs forgot, or lacked awareness of caution, and boundaries. They did not realize that zeal, and imagined embodiment of the sport's hero, cannot repair windows that got in the way.

Neither did it repair the social breaches, depending on the house owner who had to do repairs. Thanks to advancement, burglar bars[21] carried our double duties: protection against home invasion, plus protection against shattered panes, which could also shatter relationships.

What shatters your window?

Chapter 14

Shatters

Like windows, outlooks and views abounded when I was a girl. Some comments about good looking girls especially, mystified me.

"That one is going to break many hearts."

"Why do you have to be a heart breaker?"[22]Dionne Warwick asks to music.

Millions world wide, echo this question, everyday. We have all seen that happen. Hearts are like glass windows. Managing them, requires care, and caution.

Man has been breaking hearts since the garden of Eden, and we all have the potential for that.

Behaviors: missiles such as slights, rejection, and hatred, plus other behaviors that lack hospitality can break hearts and leave lives in shambles. This needs not be the case, however. Just like cleaning windows, enhances clarity, so adjusting our feelings and opinions, will help interaction, and avoid or mend broken relationships.

Window cleaning has evolved. With some types of windows, we can now stay in the same spot and clean inside and out. There's also no limit to cleaning fluids. Many opt for the commercial types, while others rely on news paper, and vinegar, or soap and water. What we use does not matter, but it matters that we have clean windows.

It requires time, effort, and energy, but gives much satisfaction. We all appreciate the glow, and the clarity that cleaning produces. A missed spot can distort viewing. Our blind spots will do that in our interactions. Commercial window cleaning has become a specialty, and in some cases, poses danger, but workers practice caution and safety through equipment.

Before workers clean residential windows, residents receive notice so that they can safeguard their privacy.

In a similar way, mending relationships has become a specialty. It includes forthrightness mixed with kindness. When, and if we see spots: flaws in others, and likewise when others see flaws in us, with potential threats to interaction, we approach each other and seek favor and cooperation to discuss and tackle the problem.

Do you need to be a window cleaner?

Chapter 15

Help me see through your window

I helped some friends with cleaning in preparation to sell their house. We spent much time on the windows. On one window, a spot, seemingly a smudge; persisted despite our scrubbing, so we finally tackled the problem, from inside and outside at the same time.

Smudges develop up from outside, and include prejudice, rejection, and hypocrisy. Smears consist of reactions to prejudice and rejection, including failure to forgive, and bitterness. Mixed with these, are misconceptions, and a sense of failure and loss. We must clean them, lest they distort our outlook and block meaningful interaction. We cannot avoid conflicts. They are a part of everyday interaction.

In fact, conflicts can stimulate interaction, if we handle them with wisdom.

Sibling rivalry exists in every culture, world-wide. Ask anyone who values honestly. Also, if anyone has a day to spare, I could talk non-stop on that subject. Anyway, out of concern, parents stimulate and encourage their warring kids to work out their conflicts without the use of physical or verbal bashings. Sometimes the verbal creates more destruction, but neither is encouraged or accepted.

One author expands on sibling rivalry. In her childhood, she and a sister often competed and bickered. One day, as the battle waged toward physical combat, their mother intervened. She equipped and assigned them to clean windows. One inside, the other outside. As each scrubbed, they vented their energy, competing to see who would do better. And as they scrubbed, they made faces at each other. They soon dissolved into giggles over the facial distortions. As they laughed, they forgot they were fighting.

As long we interact, we will encounter conflicts because of our differences. This is not necessarily negativity. Even when there is some friction, we need not focus on that. Actually, the point of friction can provoke discussion, reflection, and improvement in communication. It can be like the Negative feedback system.

Most people do not start out with any intention to create smudges. They occur, and accumulate only through misunderstanding, mishandling, and decreased communication. Both smudges and smears abound, but we must first attempt to clean our spots on our windows. Approach is crucial in tackling smudges, and requires caution. The willingness to accept the fact that interaction is two- sided, plus the willingness to build bridges, are essentials.

Some are not willing, and others cannot clean the smudges they created. A relative, a friend, a teacher, a neighbor, or colleague who's died, cannot undo the pain he/she inflicted. That one spot can minimize clarity, yet we can decide to remove them: prevent them from marring our outlook. As we do that, we practice forbearance and forgiveness. We also become more aware that we too, have the capability to create smudges, and this heightens our sensitivity to avoid it.

We cannot prevent smudges, and neither do we anticipate smears. We can, however, tackle any smears we are aware of. This will at least help us to know when smears are not the problem. Parts of my personality, combined with external situations – other's input, created and left situations which emerged and mushroomed as I entered my teen years, and even beyond. It was only after I learned to apply God's word, that I was able to face, and handle those situations. Some of them often affect my outlook and interaction, even to the present.

You have probably wondered about me; what makes me think and behave the way I do. Some have probably glanced at, or even gazed at my window, and longed to look in. Come, take a peek in my window, but first consider these questions.

Does your window need cleaning?
What are the spots: smears? smudges? Both?
Will you make the first move?

Chapter 16

Looking in

Everything that enters through windows, does not pose danger. For instance, lizards and other crawling insects can cause unpleasantness for some people, and annoyance for others. Screens would have probably helped, but the cost was a barrier for a few people. Other things do enter and pose threat, even danger. These demand attention and action.

When those who should provide security – especially for children, are the source, or part of insecurity, problems enter. Without proper intervention, or lack of it, damage including heartache and lack of trust is forthcoming.

Such was my case – like it was for many others. In fact, it was likely the case for many who were were the source of insecurity. They probably experienced insecurity themselves. It is like the blind leading the blind – a cycle of viciousness that demands attention, wisdom, knowledge, love, and patience.

My motive for opening this window, is neither for blame nor bitterness, and especially not toward my father. Rather, I am recalling, owning, and dealing with memories and behaviors. My window now has more clarity. I can now see the smears, as well I see smudges. I can, at least decrease most of the smudges. I also want to sift, and sort, and manage memories, with the hope that I may encourage some who have faced, or are experiencing similar problems. I rejoice that before he died, my father found in God, the security he needed, longed for, and sought all His life.

Many of us, especially those from Caribbean backgrounds, have probably experienced unwanted things entering our houses through windows. At one point in my childhood, I dreaded the lizards more than anything else. Whereas, they seemed to intrigue and delight my brothers, male cousins and other boys, they terrified me. Encountering lizards especially, was a nightmare, and one incident stands out.

I'd just donned my 'nightie': nightgown.

What's that fee …. ling on my back? Shriek!

Yank off. Toss.

Who screamed? Was it I?

Mothers, in addition to other miracles they do, can fly. Mine did.

"What's wrong?" Concern oozed from her.

"Something is in my nightie."

She feared nothing.

Shake, shake. A lizard tumbled out, and disappeared.

"Here. It's gone put your nightie back on."

No way. I would never again don that garment. Who knew where that lizard went.

It was many years before I finally believed that lizards were not sticking out their tongues at me.

Is there a memory you wish would not cling?

Has it left you with a feeling of caution?

Have you sought help dismiss it?

Chapter 17

Dangerous intrusions

My father's alcoholism, was, however the first, and the most troublesome intruder: the one that distorted my outlook: my window on life. Each time I saw him staggering on the public road, I donned a cloak: embarrassment and sadness, lined with anger in – camouflage. I donned it till my late teens, and both liked and hated it. Tears often befriended me.

At times, anger threw off its camouflage, on the school playground.

"Don't you mock my father!" I'd had enough of that mocker.

"What's going on here?" A teacher appeared and demanded.

"She started shouting at me Miss." My accuser spoke with conviction.

"She was mocking my father", I plead my case, hoping the teacher would understand.

I had no doubt the teacher would defend me. It was, however, only in my dream. Her next words turned off the sun. "What else can anyone expect from a drunkard's daughter?"

Night descended without warning, and something crashed. I wanted to run for shelter, but where?

In a storm and other catastrophes, home is security, but if the roof is off, and the house is down shelter must come from those who provide security. The alcoholism problem should not have bothered me like it did. It was a commonality among many men, but some were able to keep in it under cover. To this day, I struggle to find any humor in skits related to drunkenness. "Unshackled"[23]

helped and bothered me. It poked my sensitivity.

Also, to the present, caring for patients with alcoholic problems, awakens memories which I hope would stay asleep – preferably die. They're memories of ambivalence toward my father, and some of the situations which may have forced him to seek refuge in inebriation. I have a debt of gratitude for teachers, Sunday School teachers, neighbors and others, who looked out their windows, saw more than just a 'drunkard's daughter', and sent out life boats for a girl who was often drowning in fear and insecurity.

Other intrusions occurred. He always smiled. He was a walking candy store. My mother cleaned his big house with glass windows. I had no reason to worry. Until ....

"Where is your mother, Patcie? Come with me right now!"

A neighbor, one of several 'mothers' – a Godsend, was going by his office that day. Her appearance and intervention rescued, and saved me. Fear and confusion had been companions, as the person we called uncle, said things I did not understand, but did not like. Nightmares became companions for long periods afterward. That and other intrusions, like serial movies which I dreaded, but could not turn off, persisted on my mind's screen.

Chapter 18

Cracked windows

I was between four and seven years old. Childhood infections abounded. At one stage Mumps rampaged villages, and decreased Sunday school and school classes. That was my house over there.

It shrank. Okay, you want to know who are those four sufferers, and why the swaths of cloths from crowns, to under chins? I'm pleased you asked. Yes, I agree, they're pictures of misery. Those four sufferers were my younger siblings. The swaths of cloths were homemade preventative measures to try to decrease the swelling, and also to discourage the desire for chewing. You would not want to hear my siblings scream. Yes, all children are screamers, but their scream was different. "With Mumps, the salivary glands around the cheeks are swollen, puffy, and sensitive. Chewing and swallowing produce much pain."[24]

The wrappings did not curb the desire to chew. Children took liquid and semi-liquid such as porridge, but that was not enough for growing bodies. They soon forgot not to chew. Four screamers can affect eardrums and patience. Hunger pain skulked, and maintained misery. Why wasn't I among them?

My older siblings got it first, and I soon succumbed, and developed immunity. Here we are on Sunday morning. Good your imagination belt is in place.

"What are those sounds – happy noises?"

They were the bells of four denominations. Each reminded families that Sunday school would begin soon. Ah Sunday school. Me in my special dress, and happy singing!

My mother, however, had to stay home that Sunday. Who else could nurse my suffering siblings with needed patience, and effectiveness? I was ready to go to Sunday school.

"Patcie. No Sunday school today. You can go next week. Okay?"

My father tried, but pushovers soon wilt. Furthermore, he did not really mean what he said.

"I want to go to Sunday school. I don't want to go next week."

Many children, including me, at that time, seem to have built-in help especially for such times. What was it about trying to touch the sky, in time with each word – in crescendo, that delivered impact?

Whatever it was, worked that morning.

My mother intervened.

"Aagh 'Picaninees': little children. Let's ask Samnia to take her, or else we'll have no peace.

Get her red crinoline dress. That's the only one she will wear. Eat up your porridge Patice.

Samnia will soon be there. There she is."

A neighborhood girl, maybe sixteen years old, appeared.

"Samnia", My mother intercepted.

"Yes, maam"

"Have you had the Mumps?'

"Yes maam. All the family had it."

"Good. It is behind you. Except for the younger ones, who have it now, every one else in our family had it. May Patcie walk with you to Sunday school?"

"Okay, maam."

"Please give her this when Sunday school's finished." My mother handed her a package.

That day, I learned about shock at a young age, and discovered that it comes in waves. Between our house and the church compound, the first one nearly knocked me over.

That was mine, and she ate it all!

What message could I send? I had to say something. I was sure crying would help.

Ow. That hurts.

I was not sure which hurt more: the pinch, or the loss of my snack. I was sure more tears would have effect.

A woman dressed in vehemence, approached. Her dress was vehemence – her hat and shoes matched, and even her forefinger.

"Child, why don't you like Sunday school?"

Would the shock not end? That hurt nearly as much as the loss, and the pinch.

She's lying. I love Sunday school. It's just that Samnia ate my snack, I ached to explain.

What was that crumble? It was a part of my world. I wanted to hide. And what is that new thing I am looking at. Is it smear, or smudge?

Chapter 19

More cracked windows

The sight slowed my steps. Drake was up to something – something I did not like. What now? I worried. He pulled back on his sling and aimed.

Oh no, I cringed inside.

C r a c k! Broken, irregular shapes replaced the pane in the window under attack.

"Ha, ha, ha. You did it," he mocked and pointed at me, as he took off like something pulled by strings not visible to the eyes.

The woman who appeared from the backyard, seemed to dance to indignation.

"Why did you do that, you …. evil girl? You father cannot replace it."

"I did not do it, Maam", I attempted defense.

Maybe she could not hear well. She continued dancing, as indignation turned to fury, moving her faster.

"Now you are lying. That's a sin. You should know that. You go to church every day Sunday."

Couldn't she see I did not, and would not do something like that? Why was that grown-up lying? I'd appeared on site: providence for Drake, bane for me. Fear, a colleague who visited often, asked for room and board, then became a squatter.

Yet another movie. Me at eleven years old. Not that bully again. That's what some teachers call him. I also, could not fight even like a younger brother, but I could at least run almost like my big sister. I was also close to our house. Still, he outran me. Panting, I wished a grownup would come by – even a big brother. Where was even a big brother?

The bully closed in.

SCREAM, SCR...... I tried a defense, although I was not sure it would have the desired effect.

"What is this? Striking a lady? Is that how your parents train you?"

I hated the movie itself, but liked the new twist.

Gladness and relief dropped by for a visit.

Please stay relief. Go away con … fusion. I, a lady? Grownups don't lie. Is this a show that Miss is putting on? I wondered. Why couldn't I see the strings that closed this puppet's mouth? Look at his eyes grow! And what plopped his hands to his sides?

Our school principal had appeared. Did her aura say: "Respect me!?"

She got it – on and off the school premises.

Chapter 20

Window camp

For a while after, through my teens, and into my early twenties, it seemed like retrospections often dispense lies. Did my appearance invite bullying? Reality, despite its harshness, imparts truth. My father's alcoholism was like the rapids, whose current overpowered many attempts to solve the bully attacks.

Although the bully resorted to verbal attacks; my vulnerability remained. Words carry much weight.

Anxiety, fear's cousin, joined and became a squatter too. Mistrust was like a puppy. They conferred with other spots, and vetoed me looking out good windows without their input. Mistrust became spokesman.

Implications surfaced, and even God was included. I dissected songs. "O God, my father …."

God is a father? Does it mean he gets drunk sometimes? I often worried.

My emotions went to Refugee camp. It had dividends – withdrawal, the chief one. Trust and certainty were rare birds. I longed to leave with them, but they never landed long enough. I remained there till I was in my mid twenties. Then one day, my window, full of spots began to clear, as I learned to let go, and trust God more.

A truism begs for a short resurrection: "Out of the frying pan, into the fire." I went as a Nanny – a twenty-one-year-old adolescent, to a new country, and culture. One more truism, please. "She fears her own shadow." That was tailored for me. What a recipe: new country, and culture. No family, relatives, or friends – at least not yet. I dreaded some of the other ingredients like racial slurs. They were like unexpected darts that always hit the mark. They confirmed what I believed about myself, especially from enforced looking through some people's windows.

Anxiety, fear, and mistrust formed a trio. They soon became a quartet as silence joined. They persisted and became my body guards almost every time I was away from my workplace. Then one day, many of the unpleasant incidents propelled me toward dependence on God. And as I learned to trust Him more, one day, as faith and mistrust wrestled, mistrust fell, and sustained injuries. Faith invited clarity, who pled for a prolonged visit.

I thank God for His people at the first assembly I attended, and still attend. Studies and work took me away for a while, but I'm back among them. They portrayed God's love: medicine which helped to recement my faith, and helped in dealing with threatening windows, as well as re-open some I'd failed to look through for a while.

Are there childhood memories that stand out for you?
Why do they stand out?

Chapter 21

Window coverings

More often than we like, not that we want it to happen, things we'd rather bar, enter through our Windows. When I was a girl in the Caribbean, lizards perpetuated that situation. I disliked and still have zero tolerance for insects; lizards in particular. For a tomboy, who loved climbing trees, that made no sense. Lizards were a part of the landscape it seemed. We could not afford screens, so we either closed the windows, and thus fresh air, or opened them to fresh air and lizards. The latter, although chock full of unpleasantness, was the choice. They caused no harm. I just did not like them.

In the same way, we encounter situations which we'd rather avoid, or prevent. Some situations are akin to "life kicking us in the teeth", as one speaker liked to opine. Other situations cause no harm, just discomfort. However, fear and anxiety in accumulation, can cause harm. Screens would have deterred the the lizards, but cost was a deterrent for some wannabe owners. Situations we're unaware of, enter our lives and we put in screens: guards which may hinder, or hamper communication, and opportunities for growth.

In Primary school, literature, especially reading, was paramount in the curriculum. Fairy tales abounded.

"Aladdin and his lamp" stood out. It was in song form, and impressed us. We sang in innocence, and with gusto. Aladdin got what he wanted from a genie in a bottle. That tale had two windows.

Longings and dreams are without harm. My window: what sadness that many lack the awareness of the spirit that lives in certain bottles. It often allows a lot of men especially, to get what they want, while countless, children, all over the world, suffer deprivation because of that.

Another tale: 'A princess oozing beauty, met a suitor sparkling with handsomeness. He lavished attentiveness upon her. What more could she desire? They married and lived in bliss. The window?

'Happiness begins with marriage, and only pretty girls get married.' That bothered me, especially when I turned thirteen. Someone once informed me I was ugly. I had to test it. What if it was true?

Mirrors, however, especially hand- held ones, did not last long anyway. Someone soon either cracked or broke them. Moreover, glancing at one's image in parts: shards of a mirror, does not deliver the true or desired image. I either covered my mouth when I smiled, or refused to smile. I wished I at least, had 'pearly' teeth so that I would have a chance to marry. I founded an agency. I was employer, and employee.

I created windows. I harassed my mind as I viewed girls, on and off the school compound.

That one will get married. That one, like me, will not. We lack prettiness, the necessity, I concluded.

School mates in innocence, also opened other windows on the school playground. In secret, I dreaded some of the ditties. They rang with innocence, but was poison to sensitive minds. One stands out. We formed a circle. Someone walked around inside.

"Little miss Nancy went to town, to buy a pack of needles......"

Surprise, surprise. Servants, or servants' daughters could, or should do that task. Anyway.

"When she sees a pretty girl, she invites her to come close, but when she sees an ugly girl, she she closes her eyes, and passes her by": 'ignores – rejects her.'

I was not the only 'ugly' girl who was rarely, or never chosen. It hurt, just the same.

"Sticks and stones, may break my bones, but words can never hurt me." I retaliated.

That was an arch lie. I, nevertheless, sometimes yelled them either in defiance, or defence, to that, or other slights. Like countless other children, all over the world, I had my share of hurts. But whereas, fingernails, sticks and rocks, broke my skin, words, left damages and scars.

Expectations often surprise us. Some women blessed with the passport: prettiness, never marry while some without it, exit singleness. I am, however, grateful that just like we outgrow clothes, and some childhood, games, we move away from some windows.

While I continued as a Nanny, I loved reading to my charges. They all liked fairy tales. Perfection marked every page.

"And they all lived happily after."

"Never seek, or marry a mate like that."

Their mother echoed my sentiment. It was good to shut that door with permanence.

I collected lies as a child, but exchanged them for truth, as I matured. The dividends from truth can endure for a lifetime. It is like opening windows that were closed for long periods. The hinges creak, there and smears and smudges that distort view. I still, sometimes want to hold on to lies, but I am still learning to prefer truth.

I have learned, for instance, that beauty has nothing to do with looks, but rather with attitude and behaviour. The latter, not physique; reveal a person's beauty or ugliness. Some people have endowments of fine features, that attract. Some tower above others in height, and prowess. There's nothing wrong with these, but they are not the sum total of an individual. What a relief to move away from that window, that some opened, and forced me to look through. It was like opening a window in a place, from which little children can fall, and sustain injuries.

What have you collected?
What windows did you look through?
Are they still posing threats?
Do know you can move away?

Chapter 22

Rips, coverings, and repairs

Coverings are a part of many windows, and just like windows vary in type and cost, so do coverings.

For example, some curtains and blinds block out sunlight, while others filter it, thus decreasing glare.

Coverings can also add a touch of beauty, and as well, enhance privacy. And just like windows, coverings' function and effectiveness, often depend on the type and the cost.

It seems like affluence and influence are related. In my childhood days, people with affluence hung curtains, which added attractiveness, and appeal. I liked gazing at them, and envisioned some hanging at the windows in my house. A few with less, or no affluence, couldn't afford them, so the ones they hung, lacked attractiveness, and were often cover-ups. They had to, nevertheless, 'keep up with the Jones.'

Sometimes we hang curtains: behaviors and attitudes – compensations to divert attention away from that which bothers us, or from what we fear may cause people to dislike or reject us. A classmate, once hung a covering.

Smallness and functionality marked the houses in many villages. Hers was no different. The only glass window lacked most of the panes. School mates liked to visit each other's villages. During lunch break one day, a group of four accompanied her to our village. I was among, but not of the troupe.

As we neared our village, and her house, nervousness jumped to my shoulder, and refused to get down.

Why was she going to those neighbor's house? I wondered. She's afraid of dogs. He'll bite her.

Dash. Slam. Escape.

Arf, arf, arf. The dog came bounding to the gate, just as she slammed it behind her.

Something was going on. Why was she bypassing her house?

"I did not want him to dirty my uniform", my classmate 'explained'.

"Your house is nice and big", one of the visitors squealed.

Puzzlement joined nervousness, and yelled in silence: That is not her house! My classmate was on a roll.

"I am not hungry yet, but I feel like having ice cream. My uncle gave me ten dollars for my birthday. Mama does not mind how I spend it. Let's have ice cream bars, get back to school early, and study the twelve times table."

Impression grinned in victory, and marched off. Question ran up, joined puzzlement and mystery, and began to speak. I was at a loss.

I too, hung coverings. At one stage, I favored curtains. My father would chastise me, but in his heart, he would have responded with delight and surprise to imagine that he owned, not two, but "six cows." My big brother too, would have, at least in his heart, shown pride and delight that he "drove a car from down town to our gate." Dislike surged in my heart for a store clerk, and a shop keeper who often belittled my mother. I lacked power to retaliate, but I would show them.

"Morning Mrs. Proven, and Miss Good. I hope you are hearty."

"Good manners for a child, who is so destitute." It worked. At least it seemed so.

Blinds worked well too.

"Patsy, was it you who weeded the front yard? Good job", my mother praised.

I waivered between happiness and fear, and hoped my good deed would cover for repeating something about a neighbor. The consequence was something I did not anticipate.

Drapes, too, had effectiveness.

"What's wrong with you? You are always hiding, crying, and won't speak. Nobody can guess what is bothering you." Miss next door neighbor showed excellence in diagnosing. diagnosing.

"She's just seeking attention." My uncle's diagnosis too, did not lack correctness.

I liked the fact that someone paid attention. I just craved someone to make fuss made over me.

Chapter 23

Pains and hang ups

Even after salvation, I often hung coverings. It seemed I had to depend on them. For example, turning eighteen, was a sea of tumult, whose waves tossed me about and frightened me sometimes.

I'm not pretty – not even good- looking. I lack importance, I mused and fretted. Uncle Youth leader says, I am to God, but I want people to see me that way too. Ah. Papa. I wish I could say this to you in person. I feel shame when you stagger on the street after drinking. I wish I could explain that I always love you, but sometimes dislike you. Mother, along with pain, I see love in your eyes. I hate adding to your stress, especially when I complain and whine. I'm a Christian, and as such should not fight with my siblings, but I do, and that hurts you.

Often, parents, whether believers, or not; can see through our coverings.

"It's pouring. You have no covering. You are out every evening. It will take nothing away from you if you miss one prayer meeting, choir practice, or Sunday school teachers' meeting. What are you running from?"

My father's diagnosis was right on. I was on the run, but was not aware, due to smears on my window.

Not long after that, our Youth leader's wife carefronted me, after my mother sought help regarding my window. They helped me clean my widow, and open new ones. I discovered that we live the Christian conviction, not at assembly on Sundays only, but every day, and especially at home. I began to look through that window, yet I soon resumed hanging coverings. And I still sometimes do that.

I'd sensed, as a young girl, God's call to be a missionary. I, however had expectations, and over the years, especially as I exited my twenties, it seemed God would not fulfill them. While on the mission field, those unmet expectations: veiled disappointments, appeared like shadows. Perplexity too dropped by – barged in with frequency. Sometimes it overstayed. We gazed out my window together.

That window needed covering. Curtains would suit the situations. Aha. Learn, and use the language with ease. Fluency, however, refused to leave the dream stage. So, what if I unknowingly often created entertainment through my mispronunciations, or rather massacre? I now laugh too.

I just needed to maintain the second mile mindset. Eating the peoples' food – minus the pepper should do it. It was, however, not only the pepper. I cannot with honesty say I like grasshoppers. I don't mind them in their natural habitat, but whether roasted or fried, I don't want them in my mouth. It was worth it, however. Thanks, fellow missionary nurse and accomplice. It was good that we knew how to turn off our taste buds.

That curtain covered some situations, but failed in the overall struggle with honesty, when no one else could see what was going in my heart. It included learning to handle the stress of adapting to singleness in a culture where marriage is a rite of passage – a necessary one. The growing certainty of my ineligibility, was often a hurricane. It rattled my window, and ripped its coverings.

What is your covering?
Is it working?
Do you need to remove it?

Chapter 24

More Windows

When I was a teen, in some circles, people mixed up values. It seemed like propriety was either in exile in hiding. Some gushed over, and used physical appearance: often a yardstick for worth and acceptance.

Complexion: light skin in particular, plus hair length and texture were major parts of that yardstick. Those who had light complexion for example, could neither do wrong, nor fail. These blind spots abounded and produced casualties among the carriers, those who caught the infection, and even their victims became carriers In many cases, some teachers focused on, and highlighted genetic traits.

"How could that happen? She has nice, long hair."

Sometimes it was:

"How could he fail the exam? A boy with such nice, light complexion."

Even some of those who had 'significance' did not escape:

"My goodness. How did a such a dark man, and with kinky hair, become director?"

Among the better-offs, although all not all of them practiced it, station had significance.

"Have you noticed how the Propers talk with their maid?"

"Yes. Before long, she will think she's on par with them. Distinctions are diminishing. I talk with my equals, but talk to my maid."

The hapless stood by, and looked out those windows, for years. I for one, did not realize I was looking at distortions.

The majority of my forebears were slaves, but even after emancipation, vestiges of slave mentality erupted, and still infected attitudes and behaviors. That window infected me. I grew up feeling that my dark skin, and short, kinky: "bad hair", made me much of a nobody.

More signs and symptoms of the infection, oozed decades later, in Nurses' training class.

"Healthy hair has a bounce", a teacher said in innocence during a Physical Assessment class.

My hair doesn't bounce – even with the perm. It's not healthy. I do have bad hair, I groaned on the inside.

A matter-of-fact statement, full of innocence. Still, I added it to my window with the other spots. Without warning, insecurity gate-crashed, joined forces, and threatened failure in the course.

One day, insecurity over-did it, as students practiced on each other.

"You have a strange pulse", my partner informed me.

"My pulse is not strange!" Why is she putting me down? I was ready for battle.

"Why are you taking personal affront?" Bafflement twisted my practice partner's brow.

To me, it was a confirmation of windows of the past. I, in fact, had a medically confirmed extra heart beat which has never affected my health.

I could not see the world with clarity. I longed for perfection, yet I blocked the path toward it. I put up screens against any criticism. Just like I once secretly disliked the broken, wooden windows in our house when I was a child, I hated the windows I was encountering. I put in burglar bars – gave wide berths to those whom I thought opened those windows. Yet it seemed I was glued to them. I sometimes tried to slam them shut, but it seemed they were fixed. They affected relations, but in my reactions, I only created more smears.

What type of window do you have at this stage?

Chapter 25

Handling Windows

I am still learning about windows. One fact is, they're a necessity. We expect them to be open, at least sometime. After all, they promote light and fresh air, decrease stale air, and provide views. I however, must not – except in situations like a fire; or in a situation which could cause mouldiness, force any open.

If I slam a window shut, I could hurt others, and myself, rather than address issues. Furthermore, I could cause damage: ruin opportunities for interaction. I must, instead strategize, and a part of this, is window cleaning. Take yet another trek with me through my childhood: more peeks through windows.

New neighbors. I could not believe she'd moved next to me. We had issues on the school playground.

We did not, and could not see eye to eye. She did not see eye to eye with many others. One day our differences escalated into a spat. I was alone at home. It was not a face-to-face encounter. My house was above hers on the hill. I stood by my window, could down at her, and hear her, as she stood in her yard.

She could hear, but not see me. We hurled darts – concealed in words. Word war.

Whiz. Hers initiated the war.

Whiz, back. I would not be outdone!

Back and forth, the darts continued.

Bull's eye. Ouch. One of hers hit me – with force.

Whiz, whiz, whiz. I would not accept defeat.

Whiz. Whiz.

Whiz back. Oh no, I was out of ammunition that had effect. Anyway, this should work.

Slam. Ouch, again. I was a casualty.

Why hadn't I thought of that finger between the slots? I soon forgot why I tried to close window, and even the purpose of the war. Pain reigned – dart pain, and pain from slamming the window on my finger.

The gladness I felt was because she could not see me. Tears of anguish, self- pity, and anger mingled to assist me. Anguish won, and anger followed.

I can also learn from others, not to force a window open. Out of a longing to change situations, some people bang on, or throw rocks at closed windows. This can produce unexpected, and undesired results.

Yet another boy from my girlhood, exemplified this.

A neighbor lived like a hermit. Curiosity, like an itch, demanded attention from a boy from another village.

"Who's living in that house? The window is always shut. I bet there are ghosts."

Words popped out like kernels of corn from a skillet over heat.

"A woman." I hoped he was through. I was with his questions.

"What do they call her? Do you think she is inside now?"

I hoped he understood shoulder and eye language, because otherwise, he would learn nothing more. I thought he'd quitted, but two days later, I realized he'd not.

Annoyance and disapproval, two guards joined me and watched in silence.

Bang, bang, bang. The window made of metal, took a beating from the side of his fist. Then with haste, he hid and awaited the outcome.

Nothing.

Run and tell papa, I commanded myself.

Henry must have read my thoughts. His eyes seemed to bore into my mind. He also looked like a draftee for for any school's tack and field team. Cancel trying to get papa, I warned myself.

The itch must have smarted. Two weeks without attention was a lot. I arrived at a scene I did not like.

Crash. Crash. Crash. Rocks yelled at the corrugated zinc roof.

Nothing.

The urge to dash and get a grownup compelled me, but fear that he would throw one of the rocks at me without missing, rooted me to the spot. Still, I did not want to be a scapegoat again. Where were the grownups? I wished one would come by.

Crash, bang, crash.

I wished he would give up and go away, but rocks kept yelling. That time in succession: roof, window.

Wait. Someone's arriving. It's …. her! As he hurled a rock at the roof, the neighbor appeared with suddenness. She stood unnoticed, and watched in silence as Henry bent to gathered more rocks. She moved closer to the window. He rose. Intention and expectation egged him onward.

Hurl. Thud!

Gasp!

Was it mine, hers, or his? It must have been hers. She must hurt. A hand – rings on two fingers – a hand I had never seen up close, rubbed the sore spot on her right forearm.

Why didn't she cry, or at least scream? I recalled that grownups didn't cry. Had Henry become a deaf-mute? What pried his mouth open, and plopped his hands to his sides? Why didn't he run?

What's happening? Do eyes talk? I have seen young male goats do that while they lock horns in battle. They seem to be in a trance. Shut up silence.

Henry had struck – albeit without intention or malice, an old, retired teacher and widow who had hearing disabilities, and coped by withdrawing.

"S …. Sorry maam. I … did not see you co… me maam, I …. I."

Silence resumed thundering. It felt like a dream, but even in dreams, people speak, like my brother does sometimes. Silence I told you to be quiet, silence. He's leaving. I hope he does not trip. He keeps looking at her. Maybe he's worried she may grab and spank him. I wish she would do that.

Silence finally obeyed. A raven, two trees away, made too much noise.

"Henry has grown up overnight, it seems. Then again, he's now fifteen. He is maturing, still the change came with suddenness."

That teacher spoke with precision and correctness. Henry still strolled through my village, but he had become like a stranger.

Without the same offence, and even without intention, others misused their windows. Passers by had to be aware, and some even wished they could slam them shut. Who knew when someone may throw water especially? A few also, as they happened to pass by; heard, misinterpreted, and circulated things not meant for them or anyone else to hear.

Has anyone tried to force your window open, or shut?
Have you ever longed to force someone's window shut?
Have you ever thrown anything from your window?

Chapter 26

Managing Windows

We all have windows. We know they need opening and cleaning. They also need adjusting, depending on the weather. We need to handle them with care and caution. We ensure that children and pets do not climb up, and fall from upstairs windows. If there are broken panes, we remove them, or cover them to prevent getting injured.

Views and opinions are our windows. We open windows to let in air and light, and get information about what is happening. When we state our feelings, outlooks, and opinions, they can stimulate and build community, as people receive encouragement from each other. They can also cause damage, depending on how we express them.

Windows, like some in past 'sick room', need opening. That includes decreasing and getting rid of pent- up feelings of insecurity, and learning to listen to various feelings and opinions, especially those which contradict ours. Others, like mine was, for a long time, may need cleaning: getting rid of long-held fears, doubts, and misconceptions. And there are those that may need closing: owning and dismissing prejudices that devalue others. Still more cleaning may include dismissing unrealistic expectations that stunt growth.

Despite all, however, force is not the approach. We may need to force ours open, especially in situations akin to emergency such as a fire from buildups that go unnoticed, and in other drastic cases that threaten communication, and mar or destroy interaction and well being. For example, God used even non-believers to intervene in my situation, and help to force my window open. They saw spots I was not aware of, behaviors that were deterring my progress.

Close to the end of the Practical Nurse program, I hurt my back, and had to quit. I'd already missed too much practicum. In an earlier semester,

I'd run a cart over my toes. That, however, was not all. The instructor knocked on my window. Her evaluation outdid my physical discomfort.

"You need to tend to this injury, so will need time off – again. Use it as a time for reflection. Your grades are satisfactory, but nursing includes more than care giving. Feedback and criticism are essentials and you are no where close to handling them in order to function as a nurse."

In a previous semester, a head nurse made similar observations, and tried to pull the alarm:

"That young woman has potentials, but lacks readiness in interpersonal relationship. She needs at least another year to cement that, and gain maturity."

To me it was a hurricane. It rattled my window. Shatters. I failed to see that smears overruled: people just did not like me.

They were right. I had a faulty window. Nurse's training took longer. By then I was more ready. But even even then, smears continued to occasionally mar my outlook. Immaturity hung out with ignorance. Denial blinded me – denial of my weakness, and, my strength. My window needed cleaning, and adjustment.

Maturity and reality, backed by honesty, free to say that I encountered much bigotry during training, and during the early stage of my nursing career. I recall when nurses were encouraged 'not to eat their young' due to a regrettable trend, where some nurses, particularly, some close to retirement, "felt threatened" by the influx of younger, but more so, by on-white nurses. Most of my spots, were, however, smears.

God may use us to close other types of windows. I recall a blind, elderly neighbor – a widower who had no children. His bedroom reeked of mustiness. Suspicious spots marked almost every item, more so, his bed linen, and his clothes. His glass window lacked one pane, and he could not afford to replace it.

There was no protection when it rained.

A benefactress soon replaced the missing pane with board. In addition, she replaced most of the ruined items. It made a difference when everyone, including the widower could manage that window again, especially when he was able to close it against the rain.

Do you have a window that you need help to close?
Are you willing for that that to happen?
Do you need to help someone close a window?

Chapter 27

Almost like new

Before we tackle someone else's window, however, we may need to first ensure that ours are clean and clear, not perfect. If our windows have spots, we may think they're on our neighbor's. If each thinks the same, then no one can boast of perfection, but will have a desire and willingness to help each other. We do this, despite vulnerability and other risks. We're aware that open windows attract other than intended purposes. Likewise, in our interaction, there's potential for misunderstanding, disagreement, and other conflicts.

We may discover that we need to remove coverings, and even curtains, or we may need to open the curtains more, so that more light can permeate: learn about other cultural behaviors, find out why some people behave they do. When we do this, we practice patience, and genuineness in listening, even when some discoveries and revelations may shock us. This may require more than we imagine.

When we are in a room without light, for a while, our eyes adapt to the darkness, and it takes a while when to readjust to light. In the same way, it may require some adjustment for some people to understand and appreciate our views, good and sound though they may be. Vice versa, it may require much to see other's points of view. It does not mean we accept and practice what is contrary to truth. We also accept the fact that some may react with unease when we share God's truth with them.

Speaking of windows. I will open one I feared to open before, although it may be a bit late to do so.

In the book, "Irregular People," the author encourages readers to avoid those who hurt them. I see a fault in this. Yes, others do hurt us. In fact, wisdom compels us to distance children and adults from those who have hurt them in physical ways. However, in the cases of emotional slights and hurts between adults, we need to realize that without any intention, we may be 'irregular' in someone's life. My window may hurt someone.

On the subject of removing spots, especially smears, I recall when my friend and I tackled the spot on the window we were cleaning. She beckoned to me from her spot outside.

"Would you work a bit: focus on that little spot? I have used quite a bit cleaner, and scrubbed a bit, but it is still there. It seems to be on the inside."

I could not see it at first, but when I lacked no certainty, it was on the outside. My friend had an idea.

"Let's tackle it at the same time, from inside and outside?"

We resumed cleaning with vigor, and intention – more so with intention. We focused on, and tackled the spot together. They needed to sell the house, and I wanted them to have success doing it.

The spot disappeared. It either disappeared, or become so minuscule, that the glow outshone it.

Whatever the case, our focus and effort combined, produced clarity and satisfaction. It was like putting in a new window.

Are there spots you long to eliminate?
Do you long for clarity enough to clean the inside first?
Are you ready to do it?

Chapter 28

Opening up windows

No one has to be cooped up inside, except by choice, or circumstance. We cannot imagine buildings without windows, and we don't need to. Everyone has windows today. Health regulations, plus affordability ensure that everyone, not only has windows, but also, windows that function. These days too, misconceptions about air, once accepted, and practiced, are reversed. In fact, today, people everywhere, depending on the country, and the weather; make sure a window is open, at least for a while, to ensure fresh air.

It is a fact. With window's evolution, we can get air without opening some windows. We, however still need to get fresh air, and most windows can be, and must be opened for air. We cannot imagine life without interaction: an essential for community and growth, yet people some have views and outlooks they do not broadcast, because they have no opening: they're either afraid, or don't know how to do it. They therefore need an opening, so others can view their outlooks, and help with needed adjustments. Opening their windows may help others too.

Before opening some windows however, caution is a must, especially for windows starting on second floors. Bars, or other protection must be in place, lest pets, children, and even adults may fall from them, and incur injuries.

Temperaments: views and outlooks, are like the elements: sunshine, clouds, rain, and snow. Some are like storms, knocking people over in their wake. Some create smudges' just like wet leaves, and insect carcasses left to dry on window panes. They can also be like rain getting through windows left open, and without protection, casing dampness, and resulting in mouldiness.

Some people – like I did for years, react with fear, suspicion, mistrust, silence, withdrawal, and with unforgiveness. Buildups like these can be like a fire erupting with surprise. It's like releasing too much kerosene – once a staple cooking equipment in many countries. An excess of it, in the presence of the minute flicker of a struck match, can cause a fire. Oxygen would help to deter that, but my elderly neighbor exemplified what some do, when in danger: withdraw instead of getting help, thus perpetuating the problem.

No one likes unwanted things entering through our windows, so we close them. We need air, so that makes screens a necessity. Some are wary of opinions, feelings that hurt or offend, so develop mistrust and close their lives. For a long time, and even till now, doing so is a temptation. It can be like the situation where some used to imagine that air was bad for the sick. They develop sensitivity, paint over, or, or board up: close their lives, and give wide berths to those around them, just like the pandemic obligates.

Opinions can, and do offend, but not all of them. But whereas, we can use screens to bar the unwanted from entering through our windows, we do not need to bar all interaction. We can, instead learn to temper: differentiate between the ones that truly hurt, and the ones we allow to hurt us. And when we need to use screens and bars, we must choose those that work. Some we depend on, may only appear to work. We must ensure that we block the harmful, but not what is essential: growth enhancing interaction and community.

Dangers abound, and there are situations that necessitate screens, or bars. Even so, we must use the correct ones, lest we practice mistrust, close people out, and thus block interactions, which like fresh air, we all need – cannot do without. The mind is our souls' window. We broadcast what we are through our outlooks on life. Our views affect us and others. Just like we need windows for viewing, so we need each other's windows for exchange and growth. And just like everyone today has various types, so we all have various views which need opening.

Some personalities are strong, thus strong views. If not handled with caution, it can cause harm, and is akin to tossing something out a window without warning, and hurting someone, without awareness. Those views and opinions can even cause destruction. Others have personalities, and views which may seem to lack strength or popularity. They equally, need an outlet. Overall, opening our windows – airing our views produces effects which justify adjustment, including correction. All windows have similar purposes, so do all views/ outlooks.

There is Skylight, Picture, Sliding, Storm, Stained. Whatever our type, we are no longer just smoke holes.

Neither do we need to be boarded up, and neither do we need to close out fresh air, out of ignorance or fear. We're all glass window, in a world of darkness. We're also, stained glass windows, telling a story.

We draw attention because God lives in us, and we reflect His likeness. This includes love, joy, and peace.

How is your window at this point?

References

1. A song by Julie Sytner and 10/04/2017

2. Wikipedia, the free encyclopedia 10/04/2017

3. Window Wikipedia 10/04/2017

4. Brocket, Jane. 2018 How to look at stained glass. A guide to the church windows of England Bloomsbury Publishing Plc 2018

5. Joel Aigner One Studio& Fifty years of Stained Glass EWC Press

6. Merriam-Webster Dictionary and Thesaurus

7. Online Dictionary's definition of view

8. 2nd Samuel 6:20 English Standard Version

9. 2nd Samuel 6:21 English Standard Version

10. One Armed Swordman A Hong Kong wuxia film produced by the Shaw brothers, and popular in the Caribbean in the 60s

11. Wikipedia Unshackled A radio drama series produced by Pacific Garden Mission, and Broadcasted in the Caribbean in the 60s, and 70s

12. Online research. Canadian pediatric Society 23/12/2021

13. Wikipedia A monetary currency, and the British money system used in Jamaica and other Caribbean countries before the introduction of the decimal system, dollars and cents. 13/01/2022

14. Free Issue was a system in the Caribbean school system. It offered free school material to students who otherwise, could not afford it.

15. A sling used in Jamaica in the 50s, and 60s to get birds from the air. Also used by elderly people with limited movement, to scare animals and birds from vegetable gardens.

16. A spinning top once popular among boys in Jamaica, in the 50' 60s, and 70s

17. A British- influence term, used by Jamaicans to denote health and wellness.

18. "Why do you have to be a heartbreaker?" A song by the Bee Gees, released in 1982

19. A nail 7.6 centimeters long

20. Wikipedia. 17/01/2022 Merriam Webster